I see the world in motion
including "ballet class"

Madame Suzelle Poole

Copyright © Suzelle Poole 2018

All Rights Reserved

All rights reserved. No part of this publication may be reproduced, distributed, or transmitted in any form or by any means, including photocopying, recording, or other electronic or mechanical methods, without the prior written permission of the publisher, except in the case of brief quotations embodied in reviews and certain other non-commercial uses permitted by copyright law.

Title page illustration by Gregory Troik

JP illustrations by Jonathan Poole

SP illustrations by Suzelle Poole

Audio recordings by Bob Michaels

ISBN 978-1721265817

To access the audio files for this book, go to

www.readerplace.com/world

Use world as the password. Activate buttons to hear poems.

To purchase a CD, send $5 to Readerplace Books, LLC

11975 Bajada Road, San Diego, CA 92128

Published by Readerplace Books, LLC

http://www.readerplace.com

Printed in the United States

Contents

ballet class 3

watching animals 5

opera 7

last night 9

ballet 11

"s" 13

scale of eight 15

painter 17

sailor 19

pretty girl 21

I'm getting very big now 23

flower has a petal 25

a friend 27

"r" 29

to the seaside 31

at the beach 33

the stoat 35

limerick 2 37

hippopotamus	39
contact	41
birdie	43
four little ladies	45
on balcony	47
on balcony two doves	49
spring is amazing	51
on balcony	53
my balcony	55
sitting on my balcony	57
moving my chair	59
trees	61
shamrocks in our home	63
The Legend of Stone Soup	65
naptime lullaby	67
pets	69
A Mother's Day Story	71
Photographing a Squirrel	73

ballet class

I put on my tunic,

I made my hair neat.

I learned how to stand.

and turn out my feet.

I heard how the terms

came from france long ago.

I jumped and I whirled.

I pointed my toe.

I counted to music.

so difficult it seems.

to put all together

the dance of my dreams.

Gregory Troik

watching animals

have you ever watched a line of ants
march in a long, thin row
from a hole high in a wall
right down onto your toe?

after rain, on wet grass,
see an earthy worm.
watch the way he moves along;
a wriggling, rolling, squirm.

a little bird is standing,
not very far away.
he turns his head from side to side
a movement bright and gay.

I peer into the brook.
the water is so clean.
I see some fishes
swimming there,
their scales a golden gleam.

lift a rock and out may come
a crab no bigger than your thumb!
his many legs move him away.
now it's time for you to play.

opera

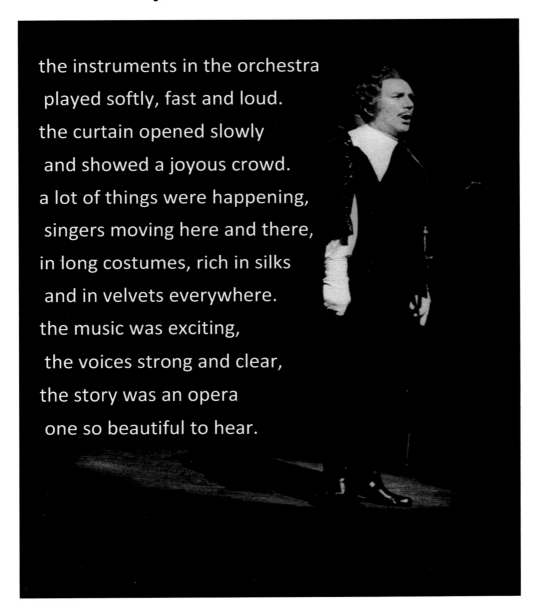

the instruments in the orchestra
  played softly, fast and loud.
the curtain opened slowly
  and showed a joyous crowd.
a lot of things were happening,
  singers moving here and there,
in long costumes, rich in silks
  and in velvets everywhere.
the music was exciting,
  the voices strong and clear,
the story was an opera
  one so beautiful to hear.

last night

lightning flashed in the night.
thunder rolled with all its might.
the rain fell down upon the flowers.
then I slept for hours and hours.

ballet

once upon a time,
the other day,
I was taken to the theatre
to see a ballet.
we sat in a seat.
we waited a while.
the music was exquisite.
quite a different style.
the curtain opened sideways
and showed a splendid scene;
some dancers moved about
in pretty white and green.
the ballet told a story.
I watched it to the end.
when the dancers came to bow
a deep and graceful bend.
we clapped with joy and awe
what a wondrous time we'd spent!
the vision had been so lovely.
I remembered...as we went.

"s"

swings and seesaws in the sun

swinging and swooshing sliding along

soaring frizbees sailing by

sand castles down swallows in the sky.

scale of eight

                                                        doh
                                            te
                                    lah
                              so
                        fah
                  me
            reh
doh
that is the scale of eight we know
it is also known as tonic-sol-fah
tra
    la
        la
            la
                la
                    la
                        la
                            la.

JP

painter

a painter with an easel
sits a long time in the sun,
looking at the scene.
painting is such fun.

JP

When I grow up
I'd like to be a sailor sailing on the sea or a soldier marching by or an airman in the sky.

sailor

when I grow up I'd like to be
a sailor sailing on the sea

or perhaps a soldier marching by
or an airman in the sky

pretty girl

pretty girl, pretty girl
all dressed in blue,
her hat, her coat
and each little shoe.

here comes a boy
with a ball and a bat.
look at him now.
he's doffing his hat.

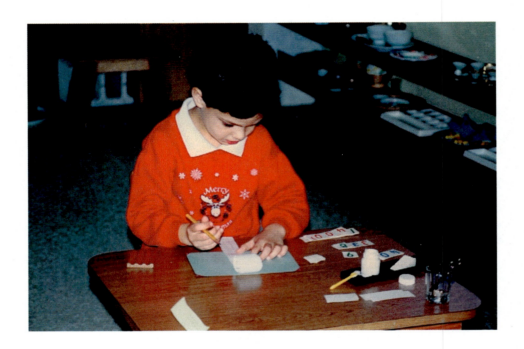

JP

I'm getting very big now

I'm getting very big now

I have a lot to do.

I know a lot of special things

which I can tell to you.

JP

SP

flower has a petal

a flower has a petal.
a pin is of metal.
water is wet.
a dog is a pet.
candy is sweet.
a child has two feet.
a yard is a length.
my arm has such strength!
much more do I know
as I learn and I grow.

JP

a friend

I like to make a friend.
that's easy now you see;
all you do is smile and say
"come and play with me!"

"r"

run robert

run robert

run, run, run.

run round the rock

having fun in the sun!

SP

to the seaside

I love to go to the beach
which is very far away.
the sand extends beyond my reach,
too far for me to say.

I see the sea, the waves of blue.
I have my spade and pail.
should I dig? (so much to do!)
or take my boat to sail?

at the beach

should I dig a hole?
or build a castle to the sky?
should I paddle in the sea
should I run as if to fly?

the stoat

the stoat (or the weasel)
are ancient, from old.
thin-bodied fur creatures
curl up from the cold.

they're fast to catch food
they bear hundred fold.
so small, underground
I can't see, but I'm told.

limerick 2

there is a young lady from leeds

who eats only a diet of weeds.

she munches and crunches

eating great bunches,

until she goes wholly to seed.

hippopotamus

a hippopotamus
can relax; no fuss.
he eats with great glee
a sausage from a tree!
he rarely eats meat
and in the river, his home,
he does from it roam.
he's quite enormous-
the hippopotamus

contact

I hear the telephone ringing
on the table near my dad.
he picks it up and then I know
that he is very glad.

he talks and then he nods
and hands the phone to me.
I speak to my grandfather
too far across the sea.

Birdie

a little boy enjoying the banks of a river
to his wonder and delight a duck's egg did discover.
knowing it was abandoned (it was all alone),
he carried it carefully along to his home.

he placed it in a box and shone a warm light.
he gazed at it fondly both day and at night.
one day a little bird's head poked up through the shell
making loud noises that showed he was well.

he grew happy and healthy and big and quite tall,
was part of the family and loved by them all.
he had toys of his own and played near the house.
his favourite toy was his own Mickey Mouse!

he was rough with his Mickey throwing him into the water.
pushing him under (seen by Susan, the mother).
"what are you doing, Birdie?" she asked.
she ducked as the toy flew past to the grass.

he followed the father wherever he went.
so many happy times together they spent.
he obeyed his commands like a well-trained bird.
was let into the home for little visits, I've heard.

he lived ten happy years, amusing at will.
when he died, they all cried and are missing him still.

7 April 2017

four little ladies

four little ladies lived in france.
they all liked to cook and all liked to dance.
they were charming and pretty and loved to give.
they knew nice people in the place that they lived.

a party for their friends was just the thing.
for them they would dance. for them they would sing.
they dusted their home- vigorously polished the wood.
they planned a fine menu and cooked tasty food.

their guests arrived. greeted them with glee.
they dined and danced together, to music, happily.

SP

on balcony

looking at my beautiful shamrocks
with lovely white flowers.
I gaze at my plants once in a while
for hours and hours!
a teeny weeny bee so small to see
flew into a blossom of white, yes, really!

to see such a sight
fills me with delight.
he stayed in the corolla
quite a long time
then flew away
the gift of knowing- sublime.

2016 November

SP

on balcony two doves

what one loves
is to see two doves
sit on my balcony
eyes to eyes with me.

they stood full of beauty
looking at me acutely.
maybe five minutes they stayed.
a visit for which I'd prayed.

their colour
and sculpture
a sight to behold.
a moment to be told.

as I write they've returned!
and then flew away.
they approve of me, maybe.
their "coos" with me stay
22 April 2016

SP

spring is amazing

I am sitting on my balcony
listening to bird sounds.
I have had wine at my elbow
now looking at my surrounds.

one tree has tiny green leaves
luscious and so amazing.
for I thank God for his dear miracles.
nothing does His fazing!

lovely plants are striving to survive.
new shoots of previous plantings
seem happy and alive!

the winter has been easy
quite kind, unknown to us.
so we should all be grateful
not complain and never fuss.

2 March 2016

on balcony

a butterfly landed on my tummy
and climbed up to my chest.
I gloried in its presence, a lovely
beauty, a message to bequest.

I've had another morning,
rich in warmth and wealth.
lovely people do surround me
and I am in fine good health.

my home and plants have pleasure
for me, when I come to view.
their leaves, and green again.
I thank the Lord for beauties, new.

14 September 2014

SP

my balcony

yesterday and today I bent 'neath lofty trees!

to settle upon my chair and gaze on sights to please.

I'm in total awe of what my beloved said to me.

my John said "the wonders of nature" as now I always see.

six weeks ago all was quite bare. again only sticks in small planters.

that was all that was there.no flowers or nice greenery. all cold and bereft.

no privacy for my home. "nothing" was left!

now flowers burst forth showing colours and shape.

green leaves emerge miraculously various and delightful. I gape.

I sit in their shades, enjoying the scene.

little birds perch above me in healthy green.

my private domain, so protected, sunshine!

I thank God for giving me this joy--mine, so divine.

30 April 2008

SP

sitting on my balcony

a beautiful sunset
of orange and gold
amazing to see
a sight to behold.

grey everywhere else
showing avocado-coloured trees.
everything is still—
not even a gentle breeze.

now the cicadas sound.
the birds still sing their song.
I love to sit and follow it all along.
a lovely song.

June 11, 2016

JP

JP

moving my chair

it is late afternoon and I hear "coos" far, far away.

reading *A Grief Observed* by C.S. Lewis again, I must say.

this morning with great gusto and with rubber gloves

I cleaned my dear balcony with its plants and its doves.

a lot had to be done 'cause they nest o'er my chair.

I cleaned everything and swept everywhere.

my chair I removed to the end of cement.

I arranged everything the way it was meant.

the middle I left so their twigs will fall

to down below and not bother at all.

April 28, 2017

SP

trees

the trees on the balcony are
showing buds and green.
they survived the freeze in winter
I'm glad their glory's seen.

31 March 2015

SP

shamrocks in our home

the shamrocks close their leaves,
as if to dream.
then open them later.
always pretty and green.

delicate white flowers
often appear
each stem has a root
making it easy to share.

I muse on its beauty
its leaves that unfold.
an unusual plant
for one to behold.

7 January 2012

The Legend of Stone Soup

They'd traveled a long way. They rode through a wood.
They were thirsty and tired. And in need of some food.

They came to a town, pleasant and neat;
They were confident, at last, for something to eat.

But, alas, the people who lived there were wary.
They'd heard about strangers being greedy and scary.

They went into their homes. They hid all their food.
They greeted the visitors, shook their heads and just stood.

The travelers were hungry and not really bad.
They talked to each other, feeling quite sad.

They asked for a caldron to boil just plain water.
They put in a stone. A crowd came to gather.

They said soup was soon ready but needed a lift.
If one had an onion, t'would be a great gift.

Onions were brought. People were curious.
They watched the clear water. Boiling was furious.

The travelers said "it needed some meat,"
To add to the stone and into great heat.

That was provided. Potatoes were found!
Carrots were brought, dug up from the ground.

Smiles then abounded, the soup smelt delicious.
As people surrounded, they passed 'round the dishes.

Now everyone was happy and trusting each other.
They ate and they danced. They liked one another.

8 July 2007

naptime lullaby

try to go to sleep.
try to go to sleep.
close your eyes
and don't peep.
try to go to sleep.

try to go to sleep.
try to go to sleep.
close your eyes
and don't peep.
try to go to sleep.

look at your books
and don't speak.
they're trying to go to sleep.

SP

SP

pets

three newborn kittens, in a flower pot.
such a delight to remember. I never forgot.
their mother adopted me, she's a lovely cat.
now they are grown, since the day they'd been begat!

close and kind in temperament, this family.
I enjoy their independence and their friendliness to me.
soft, warm and loving, stirring my emotion.
demanding my affection and giving me devotion.

11 May 2011

A Mother's Day Story

Once, there was a little boy who, one day, decided he wanted to give a special present to his mother.

He thought to himself, "I will give her one of my favourite toys- but, no, Mummy does not really enjoy playing with the toys that I like. I know she loves pretty flowers. I can give her some flowers. But no, Daddy just gave her a huge bouquet of flowers so she does not need them at the moment. Perhaps chocolates- but, recently, Mummy's not eating chocolates."

Suddenly, he thought of the best gift for his mother. He went into the kitchen where his mother was preparing dinner for everyone. "Mummy!" he waited until she looked at him. "Please bend down as low as you can." She did. "I want to give you something." He gave her a big hug.

May 1995

Photographing a Squirrel

As a young man a squirrel did find

to use as a model, this was on his mind.

At his home, he set up the scene.

He took photos all day, right into the e'en.

His mum came "John, put your squirrel away.

High tea's all prepared, now don't delay."

John said "Yes, Mum, right away I'll clean up."

He called to the squirrel and had to look up.

On the curtain and gnashing his teeth,

the squirrel would not respond to get underneath.

The cage, all ready, would not entice

or John holding tidbits with a voice really nice.

John got quite desperate (the squirrel actively bound)

saw his father arrive and called him around.

"Dad, he won't listen and go into his cage."

His father talked firmly, as if in a rage,

"Get in there!" the squirrel scrambled with fright

went into his cage. Now the family could feed!

All was all right.

                                                London

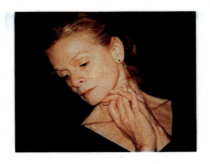

Photo by Jonathan Poole

Suzelle Poole has written poems because she needed some for the children in her classrooms. When the 2 1/2 to seven year olds enjoyed the first few poems, she was encouraged to write more, including more advanced, longer stories in poetry form. The children say them spontaneously: together and by themselves. They use them for 'research' because they remember them. Every morning, at least three children chose to find a poem to say or to display. They requested them and asked that the whole album be brought to the classroom, if it were not already there! The poems are written correctly grammatically, without fantasy and with enjoyable lessons in animal life, geography and culture.

After years of happy children saying, reading and learning with her poems, she realized that they could be of general use in classrooms and homes.

She was awarded the Golden Poetry Award by the American Poetry Society, World of Poetry, U.S.A. Mrs. Poole, A,M.I. (Association Montessori Internationale) has been teaching ballet and Montessori to children of all ages in the United States, Great Britain, Germany, and South Africa. Mrs. Poole married English Opera Singer and University Lecturer Jonathan Poole, and resides in Dallas, Texas. She continues teaching and performing.

Gregory Troik, Illustrator

Spanning more than 20 years as a professional artist, Gregory Troik's experience in sculpture and drawing includes teaching, as a professor, at the Benkov National College of Art and Design in the former Soviet Union. From 1987 his career as a successful artist led to his works being exhibited in museums in the United States as well as abroad. His works include: Public art pieces, movie set design, life drawing and sculpture.

Bob Michaels, Audio Studio

I would like to extend my deep gratitude and admiration for all his fine sound recordings.

Made in the USA
Middletown, DE
14 October 2022

12686288R00044